Canning and Preserving Soups, Stews, and Chili: A Step-by-Step Guide to Canning Delicious Food

Disclaimer and Terms of Use: Effort has been made to ensure that the information in this book is accurate and complete, however, the author and the publisher do not warrant the accuracy of the information, text and graphics contained within the book due to the rapidly changing nature of science, research, known and unknown facts and Internet. The Author and the publisher do not hold any responsibility for errors, omissions or contrary interpretation of the subject matter herein. This book is presented solely for motivational and informational purposes only.

Table of Contents

Home canning is slowly becoming a heavy-duty summer activity. However, if you grow a garden on a yearly basis, learning how to can properly is a must.

Over 10,000 years ago, during the Stone Age, humans survived by collecting seeds, nuts and whatever else they could find to store away for the winter. They also developed different methods of drying out a variety of meat and fish. In order to do this, people used natural methods of food preservation.

After fire was discovered, it was found that cooked meat tasted better than raw meat. They also found that smoking the meat before preserving it allowed for better flavor and would help preserve the meat.

During the Neolithic Age, farming originated and people began to preserve the yields of their crops. The most popular dried foods were beans, corn, and wild buffalo meat.

Salt

Salt was used as a seasoning. It was discovered that soaking meat and fish in a strong mixture of salt water kept meat fresh for a period of weeks and that packing the meat or fish in pure salt had the ability to keep it fresh for months at a time.

Fruits and vegetables were preserved in what was called "Brining Crocks." Over time, they were able to develop methods of using sugar to preserve jellies, jams and marmalades.

Fermentation

Fermentation was discovered several thousands of years ago. Therefore, beer, wine and cheese have been popular staple items in the diets of various groups of people for centuries. During this time period, fermentation developed a product known to us as vinegar. This was used to pickle fruits, meats, and vegetables.

Food Preservation

Until the 19th century, the methods noted above were used to preserve food. However, in 1804, French scientists were challenged by Napoleon Bonaparte to find a new way to preserve food for the

troops. The winner of this challenge was Nicolas Appert with his patented method of canning food.

Over time, canning methods were perfected by those who were interested in the method. Until 1856, these canning methods were used mostly by the military. In 1856, Gail Borden patented the first canned, condensed milk.

Canned Food Improvements

The Civil War pushed canned foods to the next level. This is because it was the most effective method of preserving food for the troops.

In 1858, the Mason Jar was patented by John Landis Mason. Up until this point, home canning in the average house used the same methods that were developed by Appert. Throughout World War I and II, canning became necessary due to the shortages in food and money.

As technology advanced, food became more abundant and easier to access. Technology introduced frozen foods to the public in the 1950's and 1960's. Because of this, home canning declined significantly during the 1970s, when the urge to become more self-sufficient re-developed.

Today, home canning is making its way back into the average home. This is because of the rising cost in food prices. It also helps to reduce the carbon footprint by decreasing the necessity of long distance transportation.

How Long is Canned Food Good For?

Canned food can be stored safely for up to one year at room temperature. Because of this, you should label each jar carefully. Each label should contain the contents and the "use-by" date. The most effective method I have found is to use printable labels that can be printed in bulk.

Methods of Canning and Preserving

There are three methods of home canning and preserving food. These methods are:

1. Steam-pressure canning
2. Water-bath canning
3. Open kettle canning

The method that is used to can foods depends greatly on the type of food you are processing. While most people are already equipped with the necessary equipment for the open kettle method and the water-bath method, special equipment is needed in order to use the steam-pressure processing method.

It is important that you never use shortcuts in canning. It can be extremely dangerous and can cause your finished product to be unsafe for human consumption.

Why Should You Can Your Own Food at Home?

In order to see the value of home canning, you must ignore the time that you invest in canning produce. With purchasing jars, the price of homegrown or locally-grown canned food is still less expensive than produce that is purchased at the grocery store. It can also contain more flavor since you have control over what goes into the jar.

You also have the ability to choose the produce that goes into the jar and to ensure that there are no preservatives or toxins in your food.

Over the last 170 years, there have been drastic changes in the technology associated with canning. This has helped to produce safer, higher quality product at home and take advantage of your summer crop.

Equipment Needed for Home Canning

The type of equipment you will need greatly depends on what you are canning. However, if you plan on canning a wide array of products, you should have on hand:

1. One of the best things you can invest in is a pressure canner. Pressure canners are used to can low-acid foods like vegetables and meats. If you purchase one that is a decent quality, it would also be valuable as a water-bath canner.
2. A pressure canner is the most important piece of equipment used when canning low-acid foods. Foods that are considered low acid include vegetables, meats, and some premade recipes.

You can find pressure canners at any major department store and pretty much any online department store. The ideal pressure canner is the 16 to 17 quart canner. Make sure that it comes with a quality pressure gauge and petcock. When using a pressure canner, make sure to use only quality, tested jars and lids. The best brands that are available and reusable are Mason, Kerr® or Ball® type. You should also ensure that the lids are two piece lids that are considered self-sealing. This is because the ring is reusable, but the cap is not.

You can purchase jars in a wide variety of sizes. The most popular are ½ pint, pints, and quarts. For many situations, the size of the jar can be determined by how much you want to preserve at one time. However, foods like crab and mushrooms should only be canned in ½ pint jars.

There are two types of mouths that you find on jars—narrow mouthed jars and wide mouthed jars. Wide mouthed may seem a bit pricier, but they are easier to fill, empty and clean than the narrow-mouthed jars.

You will need one timer for each canner that you are using at that time. This timer is vital to ensure that you do not under- or over-process your canning jars. This will also ensure that you process your cans long enough for them to seal and that no bacteria will build up in the jar as it sits on the shelf.

The following page contains a chart of the various items that you will need in order to successfully can food at home.

Dehydrating Fruits and Vegetables

There are multiple methods of dehydrating fruits and vegetables. This chapter is dedicated to the exact recipes for dehydrating fruits and vegetables quickly and efficiently for storage.

There are four separate methods that allow you to dry fruits and vegetables. Each has both positives and negatives, and I will outline them:

Food Dehydrator

The majority of people who dehydrate their fruits and vegetables use an electric dehydrator. There are many reasons.

1. They are consistent and produce a quality product.
2. They are high quality and reasonably priced.
3. They do not require a lot of care and are very simple to use.
4. They provide flexibility, unlike other methods.

There are requirements that your food dehydrator should have:

1. Should have a thermostatically-regulated temperature dial. It should have settings between 130 °F and 150 °F.
2. It will need to have a fan or blower to make sure that the warm air is evenly distributed.
3. It should have shelves that are made of stainless steel and a good grade of plastic.
4. It should have easy loading and unloading capabilities.
5. A high-quality dehydrator will be constructed to minimize the amount of heat loss during the process of drying.
6. High quality machines will have double-wall construction with a layer of insulating material between each wall to retain heat.

7. The external cabinets should be made of hard plastic, aluminum or steel.

8. It should have an enclosed heating element.

9. It should offer a selection of tray options (most have between 4 to 10 food trays).

10. Ensure that spare parts are readily available and these parts should be reasonably priced.

Sun Drying Fruits and Vegetables

There are lot of factors that come into consideration when you are using the sun to dry your food.

1. The temperature outside needs to be above 90 °F.

2. The humidity must be low.

3. Air pollution must be low.

4. You will need to purchase drying trays and a protective netting to prevent bugs from bothering your food.

Unfortunately, there are many disadvantages to drying your food using a sun drying method.

1. You are exclusively dependent on temperature, humidity and air quality.

2. If the climate changes from one day to the next, you will need to use a backup method to complete the process. If you do not have a backup method, your food will spoil.

3. Cooler nights the food must be moved indoors.

4. It can take 2 to 4 days to dry foods using the sun, compared to 6 to 8 hours using an electric food dehydrator.

Solar Drying

Solar dryers use the heat of the sun but at a more intense level. This method gives you a higher drying temperature, which means that your food dries faster. The faster the food dries, the quicker the microorganisms and enzymes on food will die faster.

Solar drying works by using a box that collects the sun's rays; this increases the temperature you get the affect mentioned above.

You can build your own solar dryer using various methods that are easily found online.

You have the ability to enclose your food from all sides.

Oven Drying Methods

There are many advantages of using a regular oven:

1. Not dependent on weather.

2. Regulated heat.

3. Very little to not investment.

There are more disadvantages of using an oven dyer than there are positives.

1. Drying fruits and vegetables in the oven will provide you with safe and tasty food. However, it does not provide the high quality that you would get from a dehydrator.

2. Energy costs are a significant if you are drying a large quantity of fruits and vegetables.

3. Oven must be capable of maintaining a steady temperature. You do not want the food to cook, you want it to dehydrate.

4. Using you oven for a sustained period of time to dehydrate food prevents you from using it for other purposes

If you decide to use the oven:

1. You will need to test the oven's ability to maintain a steady temperature.

2. The oven door must be left open when testing or drying fruit.

3. Using your oven thermometer to test the oven for 1 hour prior to drying, you must make sure that it maintains a temperature between 130 °F and 150 °F.

4. Temperatures on either side of the range will either cook instead of drying or cause the food to spoil.

Canning Equipment

General Canning Needs:

Magnetic Lid Lifter, Tongs, Jar Wrench, Bubble Popper/Measurer, Funnel, Jar Lifter

(Click to view on Amazon)

Cooling Rack

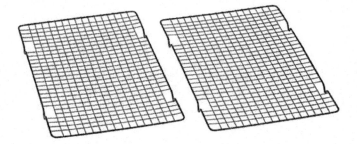

(Click to view on Amazon)

Canning Jars

(Click to view on Amazon)

Open Kettle Method:

Kettle

(Click to view on Amazon)

Sieve

(Click to view on Amazon)

Food Mill

(Click to view on Amazon)

Pressure Canning Method:

Pressure Canner and Cooker

(Click to view on Amazon)

Digital Timer

(Click to view on Amazon)

Chef's Ladle

(Click to view on Amazon)

Water Bath Method:

Water Bath

(Click to view on Amazon)

Chef's Ladle

(Click to view on Amazon)

Cutting Board

(Click to view on Amazon)

Digital Timer

(Click to view on Amazon)

Matching Lids and Bands

(Click to view on Amazon)

Pectin

(Click to view on Amazon)

Procedures for Home Canning

Before home canning season starts, you should take inventory of your canning supplies. You should also check the condition of all of your supplies. Create a list of any additional supplies that you will need in order to complete your home canning projects. It is advised to purchase these products in the off season because they are usually less expensive.

While most companies claim that their rubber seal will last for years, we recommend that you purchase a new seal for your canner annually. Pressure canners, while perfectly safe under normal conditions, are literally a ticking time bomb if the rubber seal is not in top shape.

Steps in the Canning Procedure

1. Before you begin, read the Directions for your jars, canner, and recipe carefully.
2. Pull together all of your equipment so that you can work efficiently and effectively.
3. Wash all of your canning jars, lids and rings in warm, soapy water. Rinse them thoroughly. After they have been washed, run them through the dishwasher to sanitize them.
4. Place a pan of hot water on the stove to simmer for the lids and rings.
5. When preparing your jars, make sure that you do not clean more than what can fit into one canner load, unless you plan to use more than one canner at a time. Pack jars according to the manufacturer's directions and add your liquid accordingly.
6. Use a rubber spatula to remove air bubbles from filled jars, especially if you have jars filled with loose vegetables or meat. This is a very important step. Not only does it reduce the amount of darkening when the food is processed, it also prevents the water from falling below the recommended level.

7. Make sure to wipe the rim of all jars completely clean with a paper towel or lint-free cloth.
8. Process jars once for the time recommended by the recipe or the manufacturer.
9. After the processing time is over, allow jars to cool on cooling racks.
10. Wipe the jars clean with a damp rag. Label all of the jars with the contents and use by date. Store in a dry, dark location to ensure that the food stays fresh and does not lose color as it sits.

    *** Never take them out of the canner and place them on a cold surface, the jar could explode.

    *** Do not turn the jars upside down at any point.

    *** Food may continue to boil inside the jar for up to one hour due to the pressure.

    *** As the jars cool, you will hear popping or pinging sounds. This is perfectly normal as it is the jar sealing completely.

    *** After 12 hours, test the jars for a seal. Tap on the top of the lid. The center should be dipped in and should not spring back at all. If it does, then the jar did not seal. Repack the contents with a new lid and process it again.

    *** Never re-use self-sealing lids.

    *** If the product does not seal after the second time, place it in a Ziploc® bag, label it and freeze the contents.

Altitude

Your altitude is just as important as your equipment. If you live 1,000 feet above sea level, you will need to adjust your processing time. If you fail to lengthen your processing time, you will end up with an improperly processed food that may not be safe to eat.

This is the number one reason people end up with spoiled food, mold, bacteria and harmful microorganisms in their canning jars. These may or may not be detected by sight or smell. Ingesting the food can result in food poisoning. Because of this, we have provided a chart so that you can properly adjust your processing time according to your altitude.

Altitude Chart

Boiling Water Canning

Normally, the processing times given are designed with standard guidelines. Unfortunately, most recipes are designed for use under 1,000 feet. This chart will help you to adjust the time needed for processing.

Altitude (feet)	Increase Processing Time	Altitude (feet)	Increase Processing Time
1,001 to 3,000	5 minutes	6,001 to 8,000	15 minutes
3,000 to 6,000	10 minutes	8,001 to 10,000	20 minutes

Preserving Color and Flavor in Home Gardening

In order to maintain the right color and flavor of the food you are canning, you must start with quality food and follow the process of hot packing, especially when it comes to acidic foods. Do not allow prepared food to be exposed to air. They should be canned as quickly as possible after they have been prepared.

Peeled fruit must be soaked in a solution of 3 grams ascorbic acid in 1 gallon of ice cold water. Ascorbic acid can be found in various forms.

- Powder Form – This product is available online and seasonally. Add 1 tsp to 1 gallon of water and stir.
- Vitamin C tablets – 500 mg tablets can be dissolved in water. Dissolve 6 tablets per gallon of water and stir.
- Commercially Prepared Mixes – These are prepared by mixing ascorbic and citric acid. This is available online and seasonally at department stores. Since these are different, you must follow the manufacturer's directions.

Why Hot Packing?

Fresh food is comprised of between 10 and 30 % air. The quality of your food depends on how much is removed during processing. Raw food should be packed using the hot packing method.

Hot packing involves prepared but unheated food. This is especially true with fruit. The air that is trapped around the food will cause discoloration in a period of 2 to 3 months.

Hot packing involves heating food to the boiling point and allowing it to simmer for only 2 to 3 minutes. Pack the food into jars at the boiling temperature. This will prevent air from staying in the jar, keep fruit from floating, and improve the shelf time of the food.

At first, the hot pack method may leave the fruit looking no different than the raw pack method, but after being in storage for a while, you will notice the difference.

Always follow the directions in a recipe, even if it tells you to raw pack, as they have all been tried and proven.

Soups, Stews, Chowders and Chili

Ingredients

4 lb beef chuck boneless
¼ cup vegetable oil
3 cups onion, diced
2 garlic cloves, minced
5 tbsp chili powder
2 tsp cumin seed
2 tsp salt
1 tsp oregano
½ tsp pepper
½ tsp coriander
½ tsp red pepper, crushed
6 cups canned tomatoes, diced and not drained

Directions

1. Cut meat into ½ inch cubes, removing as much fat as possible.

2. Brown meat cubes in hot oil until lightly brown.

3. Add in garlic and onions, continuing to cook until soft but not brown.

4. Add the remaining spices, cooking for an additional 5 minutes.

5. Stir in the tomatoes and bring the mixture to a boil. Reduce the heat and simmer for 60 minutes, stirring occasionally.

6. Ladle the chili into jars leaving 1 inch headspace and removing any air bubbles.

7. Place the lid on top of the jar and twist on ring until snug.

Process in a pressure canner for 1 hour and 30 minutes with 10 lbs of pressure applied

Check the chart to find out what pressure to use for a higher altitude

Remove jars and let cool and seal

Ingredients

1 lb beans, great northern, dried
1 lb sausage, chorizo
1 lb potato, diced
1 cup celery, diced
1 cup onion, diced
1 head garlic, peeled and finely chopped
10 cups chicken stock
1 bunch kale, washed and stems removed
salt and black pepper
2 to 3 tbsp hot sauce (optional)
heavy cream

Directions

1. After washing and sorting your beans, let them soak overnight.

2. Rinse and drain them to make sure they are completely clean.

3. Cook the chorizo in a large pot on medium heat. As it cooks, break it up into smaller pieces. Remove the chorizo and set to the side, leaving the grease in the pot.

4. Sauté the onions, garlic and celery in the chorizo grease for 5 to 10 minutes.

5. Take the kale and tear it so that there are rough, small pieces and set them to the side.

6. Place the mixture of vegetables in with the beans and chicken stock. Bring to a boil, setting the heat on high and boil for 20 minutes or until the beans soften.

7. Add the chorizo, potatoes and kale, stir well, bringing back to a boil. Boil the mixture for another 10 minutes.

8. Season the soup to your liking with salt and pepper. You can add your favorite hot sauce at this point if you want.

9. While boiling, you can now ladle the soup into jars and place the lid on top and twist on the ring until it is snug.

10. Place the jars into the pressure cooker

Process for 1 hour and 30 minutes for a quart

Serving

Bring soup to a simmer on medium-high heat, stirring in 1 cup water, milk and heavy cream per quart. Simmer and mix through.

Barley and Beef Vegetable Soup Mix

Ingredients

3 cups barley, pearl
3 tsp basil, dried
3 cups split peas, dried
1 ½ tsp oregano, dried
12 tbsp bouillon, beef granules
6 bay leaves
1 ½ tsp black pepper

Directions

1. Mix all the ingredients and separate them into six portions.
2. Add 2 tbsp of bouillon to each of the portions.
3. Follow the same instructions with the barley and the beans.
4. Blend the beans and spices and put them into elegant jars or gift bags.
5. Put a gift tag on the jar or package: Barley and Beef Vegetable Soup Mix, follow these directions:

Serving

Ingredients

2 tbsp oil, vegetable
1 lb beef meat, beef
6 cups water
1 package Barley and Beef Vegetable Soup Mix
3 carrots, chopped
3 stalks celery, chopped
3 to 4 potatoes, chopped

Directions

1. Heat the oil in a large stock pot, add the meat cubes and brown them on all sides.

44 | P a g e

2. Add the soup and water to the stock pot and allow it to boil, minimize the heat.
3. Cover and allow it to simmer for forty five minutes.
4. Gently stir in the celery, potatoes and carrots.
5. Cover and allow it simmer for an hour and then throw away the bay leaf.

Confetti Bean Soup

Ingredients

14 lbs beans (assorted), dried peas and lentils:
    black beans
    pink beans
    lentils
    lima beans, baby
    black eyed peas
    kidney beans, red
    split beans
    pinto beans
    red beans and white beans, small
    great northern beans
12 cubes bouillon
12 bay leaves

Directions

1. Put ¼ cup of each species of beans in the jars and layer them as you add them.
2. Select the good looking beans and put them on the bottom layer of the jar.
3. Put 8 layers of ¼" of each type of bean in the jar and put a bay leaf and a bouillon cube on top of the beans in every jar.
4. Close every jar using rings and lids.

5. Print 2 copies of the tags with recipe instructions provided.

Serving

Directions

1. Put the bouillon cube and bay leaf and select the best method to soak the beans.
2. Sort and rinse the beans in a big pot and add 6 to 8 cups water.
3. Boil at a rapid level for two minutes and then remove from the heat.
4. Cover and allow it to stay for an hour.
5. Drain the water and rinse the beans.
6. Soak overnight: rinse in large pot and add 6 to 8 cups cold water and allow to them to sit for an hour.
7. Cooking: put the beans in a large pot and add 6 cups water.
8. Add 1 can of the juice from chopped tomatoes.
9. Add one bay leaf and bouillon cube.
10. Simmer for about two hours until the beans are tender.
11. Season to taste with salt and pepper.

Ingredients

¼ cup beans, garbanzo, dried
¼ cup lima or navy beans, dried
¼ cup pinto or red kidney beans, dried
¼ cup split and whole peas, dried
3 tbsp onion, dried and minced
2 tbsp barley, pearl
2 tbsp celery flakes, dried
2 tbsp bouillon, beef granules
1 bay leaf
½ tbsp basil, dried and crushed
dash salt

Directions

Mix all the ingredients in plastic bag and seal tightly. Add recipes below to the gift.

Serving

Directions for Basic Hearty Bean Soup

1. Mix the contents of the package with 7 cups water in a 3 qt saucepan.
2. Boil and then minimize the heat; cover and allow it to simmer for 2 minutes.

3. Remove from heat, cover and allow it to sit for one hour.
4. Bring the liquid and beans to boiling and then reduce the heat. Cover and allow it to simmer for two hours until the beans get tender.
5. Toss the bay leaf and season it to taste.

Directions for Meaty Bean Soup

1. After step #3, add smoked pork hock and allow it to boil; minimize the heat, cover and allow it to simmer for one hour.
2. Remove the meat, chop it coarsely, and add it back to the soup. Remove the bay leaf, add a chopped carrot and cover to simmer for half an hour, and then season to taste.

Manhattan Clam Chowder

Ingredients

2 dz large clams
2 large onions, diced
1 cup celery, chopped
2 cups tomatoes
4 cups water
salt and pepper to taste
¼ lb salt pork, diced
1 carrot, diced
1 bell pepper, green, diced
2 large potatoes, peeled and diced
½ tsp thyme
flour

Directions

1. Steam clams in a small amount of water until they open.

2. Reserve the water and mince the clam meat.

3. Brown salt pork in a large kettle. Remove the cracklings from the fat.

4. Brown onions, carrot, celery, and bell peppers in the fat.

5. Add tomatoes, potatoes, water, seasonings, clams and clam cooking liquid.

6. Thicken the liquid with a little bit of flour.

7. Bring liquid to a boil.

8. Pour chowder into jars. Wipe the rims and place the cap on.

Process in a pressure canner under 10 lbs of pressure

Process quart jars for 1 hour and 40 minutes

Ingredients

5 lbs beef, ground
2 cups onions, chopped
2 cloves garlic, minced
6 cups tomatoes, cooked
½ cup chili powder
1 ½ tsp salt
1 red pepper, hot
1 tsp cumin, seed

Directions

1. Brown the ground beef in a nonstick kettle.

2. Add the onions and garlic and continue cooking over low heat until the onions and garlic are tender.

3. Add all remaining ingredients and allow to simmer for 15 minutes.

4. Skim off excess fat and pour into jars. Leave 1 inch headspace at the top of the jar.

Process jars under 10 lbs of pressure for 1 hour and 30 minutes

Check the chart to find out what pressure to use for a higher altitude

Serving

Warm the chili and add a can of pinto beans while it is warming. Heat thoroughly and simmer for at least 5 minutes.

Chili Sauce

Ingredients

4 qts tomatoes, cored, peeled and chopped
2 cups onions, chopped
2 cups sweet red peppers, chopped
1 hot chili pepper
1 cup sugar
3 tbsp salt
3 tbsp pickling spices
1 tbsp celery seed
1 tbsp mustard seed
2 ½ cups white vinegar (5 %)

Directions

1. Boil tomatoes for no more than 1 minute. While still hot, place in a bowl of ice water. This will allow the skin to release and come off with ease.

2. Cut the tomato in half, length wise, you should be able to shake most of the seeds out. Drain the tomatoes and keep the juice to the side.

3. Chop the onions and peppers and leave the chili peppers for later.

4. Finely dice your hot red chili pepper.

5. Combine tomatoes, chopped onions and red peppers, hot diced pepper, 1 cup sugar and salt. Simmer for 45 minutes, stirring occasionally.

6. Tie the 3 tbsp pickling spices, 1 tbsp celery seed and 1 tbsp mustard seed into a spice bag and place it in the simmering mixture. Boil the mixture until reduced by half.

7. Simmer on low to medium heat and add in the vinegar reducing the mixture to the thickness wanted.

8. Remove the spices and fill the jars, leaving ¼ inch space from the top. Place the lid on and twist the ring until snug.

9. Place the jars in a boiling water, bath keeping the water 1 to 2 inches above the jar tops.

Process for 15 minutes for pint sized jars

Also adjust if you live in a higher altitude

Remove the jars and place them on a flat surface to cool and seal

Ingredients

3 cups pinto or kidney beans, dried
5 ½ cups water
5 tsp salt
3 lbs beef, ground
1 ½ cups onion, chopped
1 cup peppers, chopped (your choice)
1 tsp black pepper
3 to 6 tbsp chili powder
2 qt tomatoes, crushed or whole

Directions

1. Clean the beans by soaking them in water for 12 hours.

2. Combine beans into 5 ½ cups fresh water and 2 tsp salt. Bring the mixture to a boil, reduce heat and simmer for 30 minutes. Drain and dump the water.

3. Brown ground beef, peppers and chopped onions. Simmer for an additional 5 minutes but do not thicken.

4. Pour the mixture into jars, leaving 1 inch headspace.

5. Place lids on top of the jar and screw on the ring until snug.

Place jars in pressure canner for 75 minutes with 11 lbs pressure for pint jars

Ingredients

2 cups navy beans, dried
½ cups onion, chopped
1 cup peeled potatoes, diced
4 oz salt pork, chopped
1 carrot, thinly sliced
salt and pepper to taste

Directions

1. Wash beans in cold water. Ensure that there are no small rocks inside the beans. Cover with water and allow them to soak for at least 12 hours.

2. Add in pork, vegetables and seasoning, bring to a boil.

3. Reduce heat and allow to simmer for 2 hours.

4. Press vegetables through a sieve and return them to a kettle.

5. Pour soup into jars.

Process jars under 10 lbs of pressure for 1 hour

Onion Soup Mix

Ingredients

3 bouillon cubes, onion, crushed
1 bouillon cube, beef, crushed
2 tsp cornstarch
1/3 cup onion, flakes
2 dashes pepper

Directions

Mix all of the ingredients in a jar and store in a dry cool place.

Serving

Ingredients

4 cups water, cold
1 tbsp butter

Directions

1. Empty the mixture into a pot and gradually stir in 4 cups cold water and 1 tbsp of butter.
2. Allow it to boil, minimize the heat and cover it, simmer for twenty minutes.
3. Ladle soup into oven-proof bowls and sprinkle with toasted bread.

Onion Dip

Blend one package of the onion soup with two cups of sour cream; chill before serving.

Ingredients

½ cup of macaroni, small shells
¼ cup lentils, dry
2 tbsp parmesan cheese, grated
1 tbsp onion, dried and minced
1 tbsp bouillon, chicken granules
1 tsp parsley flakes, dried
½ tsp oregano, crushed and dried
garlic powder

Directions

Combine all the ingredients in a container and seal it tightly.

Serving

Ingredients

3 cups water
Pasta Shell Soup Mix

Directions

1. Mix all the ingredients with 3 cups water in a 3 qt saucepan.
2. Bring to a boil, minimize heat and cover; allow it to simmer for 40 minutes.

Split Pea Soup in a Jar

Ingredients

2 ½ cups split peas, green
2 ½ cups lentils
2 ½ cups barley, pearl
onion flakes
½ cup celery flakes
½ cup parsley flakes
1 ½ tsp thyme
1 ½ tsp pepper, white

Directions

1. Combine all the ingredients and store in a tightly-sealed jar.
2. Stir before using.

Serving

Directions

1. Mix 1 cup of the soup mix with 4 cups water.
2. Add 1 cup of chopped, cooked meat and allow it to boil.
3. Minimize the heat to low and cover the pan.
4. Allow it to simmer for 45 minutes until the peas get tender.

Palouse Soup Mix

Ingredients

2 ½ cups split peas, green
2 ½ cups lentils
2 ½ cups barley, pearl
2 cups macaroni, alphabet
onion, flakes
½ cup celery, flakes
½ cup parsley, flakes
1 ½ tsp thyme
1 ½ tsp pepper, white

Directions

1. Mix all the ingredients and store in a tightly-sealed jar.
2. Make sure that you stir it before you use the mix.

Serving

Directions

1. Mix 1 cup of the soup mix with 4 cups water.
2. Put 1 cup of chopped, cooked meat in the soup and allow it to boil.
3. Minimize the heat to low and cover the pan. Allow it to simmer for 45 minutes or until the peas get tender.

Ingredients

5 lbs stew meat
3 qt potatoes, peeled and cut into cubes
3 cups celery, chopped
1 tsp thyme
2 qts carrots, sliced
3 cups onions, chopped
1 ½ tbsp salt
½ tsp black pepper

Directions

1. Cut the stew meat into 1 ½ inch cubes. Brown the beef in a small amount of fat.

2. Combine beef, vegetables and seasonings into the kettle. Cover with water.

3. Bring to a boil.

4. Pack into jars, leaving 1 inch of headspace.

5. Clean the rim and cap the jars.

Process quart jars under 10 lbs of pressure for 1 hour and 15 minutes

Ingredients

2 (16 oz) cans tomatoes, stewed
1 can corn, whole kernel
1 can corn, creamed
1 can chicken
1 can barbecue pork
1 can barbecue beef

Directions

1. Open and empty all the cans and juice into large stock pot.

2. Cook on medium heat for 1 hour.

3. Place contents into a jar, place a lid on top and screw on the lid until it is snug.

Place in a boiling water bath for 10 minutes with water at least 1 inch over the jars

Remove and place somewhere flat where it can cool and seal

Ingredients

1/2 cup olive oil

2 eggplants, peeled

1 clove garlic, crushed

2 large Spanish onion, peeled

3/4 cup celery, finely diced

2 cups tomato puree

1/3 cup green olives pitted and chopped

1/3 cup black olives, pitted and chopped

1/4 cup capers, drained

1/4 cup red wine vinegar or white wine vinegar

2 tbsp brown sugar

1/2 tsp salt

1/2 tsp pepper

1/2 tsp oregano, dried

1/4 tsp thyme, dried

3 tbsp parsley, minced

Directions

1. Pour 5 tbsp of olive oil into a stockpot and heat. Add eggplant to the stockpot, cut into 1 inch cubes. Stir fry the oil and eggplant in the pot until it is a golden brown.

2. Add in the onions, remaining oil, garlic, and celery and stir fry 10 minutes longer.

3. Mix in the rest of the ingredients, reduce the heat to simmer for 1 hour and cover, stirring occasionally.

4. Remove the lid and cook until the mixture thickens.

5. Ladle the Caponata into jars, leaving 1 inch of headspace.

6. Place lid on the top and twist on the ring until snug.

Pressure cook a pint jar at 10 lbs pressure for around 30 minutes

Cabbage and Beet Soup

This recipe makes approximately 4 quarts.

Ingredients

2 heads cabbage, shredded
1 gallon chicken stock
5 cups beets, cooked and diced
2 tsp salt
2 onions, diced
1/2 tsp black pepper

Directions

1. Combine the ingredients in a large kettle. Bring to a boil.
2. Once boiling, pour into hot jars.

Process under 10 lbs of pressure for 30 minutes

Tomato Soup

Ingredients

½ bushel ripe tomatoes
¼ tsp red pepper flakes
6 onions, diced
2 tbsp salt
2 tbsp celery seed, dried
1 cup butter or margarine
1 cup granulated sugar
1 cup all-purpose flour

Directions

1. Combine the tomatoes, onions, and celery seed in a large kettle. Boil the soup over heat. Strain soup and add seasonings.

2. In a skillet, melt butter, add flour and stir vigorously to make a roux. Add roux to mixture and simmer for 20 minutes.

3. Pour soup into jars. Wipe the rim of the jar and tighten lid lightly.

4. Seal the jars and process.

Process for 30 minutes under 10 lbs of pressure

Ingredients

¾ cup red beans, dried
¾ cup great northern beans, dried
¾ cup lentils (red or yellow to add color)
¾ cup black beans, dried

Spices
2 tbsp onion flakes, dried
2 tbsp bouillon granules, beef
2 tbsp parsley flakes, dried
2 tsp dried basil
2 tsp lemonade drink mix
1 ½ tsp chili powder
1 tsp garlic powder
1 tsp pepper
1 tsp oregano, dried

Directions

1. Layer the beans and lentils in a jar in the order listed.
2. Place all spices in a Ziploc® bag and place the bag on top of beans.

Serving

Ingredients

8 cups water
1 15 oz can crushed tomatoes

Directions

1. Place seasoning bag to the side and rinse beans by placing in a microwave-safe bowl with water that is 1 to 2 inches above the beans.
2. Loosely cover the bowl and microwave for 15 minutes.
3. Drain the beans and rinse thoroughly.
4. Place beans in a large pot with 8 cups water, 1 can crushed tomatoes and the seasoning bag you removed from the jar.

Cover the pot and bring the contents to a boil; lower the heat to a simmer and keep pot covered. Simmer the soup for 1 ½ hours or until the beans are tender, stir every so often.

Curried Lentil Soup

Ingredients

1 lb lentils, red
salt
6 tbsp onion, dried and minced
2 tbsp curry powder
1 tsp garlic powder
1 lb lentils, green
½ package apple rings, dried
2 tbsp parsley leaves, dried

Directions

1. In the bottom of each glass jar, place ½ of the red lentils.
2. Top with 1 ½ tsp salt, 3 tbsp dried onion, 1 tbsp curry powder and ½ tsp garlic powder.
3. Next, place ½ of the green lentils, ½ cup of the apple pieces, and 1 tbsp parsley.
4. Seal the jar tightly.
5. Store in the pantry for up to 1 month.

Ingredients

6 cloves garlic, coarsely chopped

1 lemon zest

3 tbsp sea salt, ground

6 bay leaves

3 tsp black peppercorns

1 ½ lbs small whole fish (smelt, herring, etc.)

2 cups water, non-chlorinated

2 tbsp sauerkraut brine

Directions

1. Mix lemon zest and garlic with the sea salt.

2. Rinse the fish and cut it into ½ inch pieces. Throw the pieces of fish (all of it) into the sea salt mix.

3. Add the bay leaves and peppercorns into the mix and fit it into a 1 qt jar, pressing on the ingredients to press the juices out.

4. Pour the brine from the sauerkraut and any extra water in the jar to finish submerging the fish. Make sure to leave 1 inch headspace.

5. Cover tightly and let sit for 2 to 3 days at room temperature. After 2 to 3 days, move to your refrigerator, let sit for 4 to 6 weeks.

6. Double strain through a sieve and get rid of any solids. Pour back into glass jars to sit in the refrigerator for 6 months.

Ingredients

½ cup butter

1 onion, grated

6 cups milk

1 pint oysters with liquor

1 cup cream

1 tsp sea salt

pepper to taste

Directions

1. Sauté the grated onion in butter in a stock pot.
2. Add the milk with the salt, pepper and oysters with liquor and cream. When adding these ingredients, don't allow to boil.
3. In order to can, you ladle the oyster stew into a quart jar.
4. Place the lids on top and twist on the ring until snug.

Place into the pressure canner for 75 minutes with 11 lbs of pressure

Always check altitude to see if this changes or not for your area

Ingredients

16 oz package split peas
8 cups water
1 large onion
4 medium carrots, diced
4 stalks celery, diced
1 cup ham, diced
1 bay leaf
4 cloves garlic, minced
1 tsp salt
1 tsp pepper
½ tsp sage
1 tbsp olive oil

Directions

1. Pour a tablespoon of olive oil into a stainless steel pot and start sautéing onions, carrots, and celery. Sauté until the onions are tender and add garlic, sage and bay leaf.

2. Rinse peas and pick dark peas and rocks out.

3. Add the water and peas to the veggie mix and cook for about 1 hour, stirring frequently until soft.

4. Cut ¼ inch cubes out of the leftover ham and cook 20 more minutes, stirring frequently.

5. Remove bay leaf.

6. Ladle soup into jars, leaving 1 inch headspace and remove air.

7. Place lid on top and twist on ring until snug.

Place the jars in the pressure canner with the pressure at 10 lbs

Quart jars really need about 90 minutes

Ingredients

½ cup butter
1 stalk celery, minced
1 small onion, minced
¼ tsp cayenne pepper
¼ tsp marjoram, dried
3 tbsp flour
3 ½ cups milk
2 cans soup, condensed cream of potato
1 ½ lbs shrimp, scallops, clams and crab

Directions

1. In a 3 quart saucepan, melt butter on low heat. Sauté onion and celery until tender.

2. Add the thyme, cayenne pepper, flour and marjoram, stirring until smooth.

3. Stir in condensed soup and mix until the mixture is hot.

4. Clean and cut seafood to the size desired. Add seafood and stir on medium heat until seafood is cooked thoroughly.

5. Ladle chowder into jars while hot and place the lid on top of the jar, twisting the ring on until snug.

Place the jars into the pressure canner for 75 minutes with 10 lbs of pressure

Remove and place somewhere to cool and seal

Ingredients

2 (14 oz) cans tomatoes, diced and un-drained

1 large onion, chopped

4 cloves of garlic, pressed

2 tbsp oil, olive

2 large carrots, chopped

2 celery ribs, chopped

1 turnip, chopped

2 cups green beans, cut to 1 inch

6 cups chicken broth

¼ head cabbage, chopped

½ tsp thyme

2 small russet potatoes, peeled and chopped

salt and pepper

Directions

1. Heat 1 tbsp olive oil on medium high heat in a large soup pot. Add onion to the pot, cooking until mostly translucent.

2. Add the garlic and sauté but don't let the garlic brown.

3. Add in all the chopped veggies and sauté for 1 to 2 minutes, using the extra tbsp of olive oil.

4. Add the salt, pepper and thyme.

5. Place the sauté mixture and tomatoes with broth into the crock pot. Cook the mixture on low for 7 to 9 hours.

6. Mash some of the potatoes to help thicken the soup.

7. Ladle the soup into quart jars, placing the lid on top and screwing the ring on until snug.

Place in pressure canner for 75 minutes with 10 lbs of pressure

Adjust for altitude as needed

Remove from pressure canner set to the side to cool and seal

Meat Stock

This recipe works for both beef and poultry stock.

Ingredients

whole chicken or turkey carcass

Directions

1. Crack the bones open to help extract flavor. Use whole chicken or turkey carcass if you are using poultry.

2. Cover the bones with water.

3. Add celery stalks, 1 onion cut into quarters, salt and pepper.

4. Allow to simmer for 1 to 2 hours.

5. Pour through colander to separate the broth from the bones and vegetables.

6. Pour broth into hot jars, leaving ½ inch headspace at the top of the jar.

7. Place lids on the jars and process.

Process under 11 lbs of pressure

Process pints for 20 minutes

Process quarts for 25 minutes